Mowing

Mowing

Marlene Cookshaw

Brick Books

Library and Archives Canada Cataloguing in Publication

Title: Mowing / Marlene Cookshaw.
Names: Cookshaw, Marlene, author.
Identifiers: Canadiana (print) 20190111194 | Canadiana (ebook) 20190111208 |
ISBN 9781771315159 (softcover) | ISBN 9781771315173 (PDF) |
ISBN 9781771315166 (HTML)
Classification: LCC PS8555.O573 M69 2019 | DDC C811/.54—dc23

We acknowledge the Canada Council for the Arts, the Government of Canada
through the Canada Book Fund, and the Ontario Arts Council for their support of
our publishing program.

The author photo was taken by Mitchell Parry.
The book is set in Scala.
The cover image is from iStock.
Design and layout by Marijke Friesen.
Printed and bound by Coach House Printing.

Brick Books
431 Boler Road, Box 20081
London, Ontario N6K 4G6

www.brickbooks.ca

for Mitch, companion-in-farms

Contents

III

I

Moving House

For each of us, there is a place from which our night-dreams
proceed and around which our mental faculties take shape.
—Roo Borson

That's it: mine's lost. Every dream
occurred in that small city yard,
even tinier brick house: worlds

it contained, and histories.
But only one future, and we all
moved away from it. For years

in dreams I brought friends home,
aligned who I met with where I
came from, made something new. I believed

the figures of my parents
diminished
this way, became human sized.

&

The owner of the Victoria Hotel, which
I don't recall but must have seen,
was interviewed this morning, having sold

the building after living in it all his life.
He has a snap of his mother on the roof
holding him when he was eight months old. Here

is a man who has not lived alone, meaning
with fewer than hundreds, since the hotel opened
in June '65, when he was one. In October

he will sign it over to a mainland firm;
they will break it into condos. He says
he's never known the building without

people in it, cars in the lot, the elevator
going up and down.

&

In the middle of the day I walk with the dog
to my aging ex-in-laws for tea.

Tom studies the phone book for the name
of the shop that used to be Radio Shack
while Muriel and I point out birds

through the sliding doors. She tells me
about the pair of pigeons—she calls them
peacocks—that visit every afternoon. Like Tom

she's dressed in eggshell blue and beige.
Frailer each week in extremity, the two
are softer, and round in the middle.

&

It's 5:45 and the sun's heat has weakened.
I pull on my hoodie and zip it.
The Zephyr squash is a dome of green

that would easily house a child. Again I
move the hose. Squash, squash, pear is day one.
Then, four beds in the greenhouse.

On the third day, sunflowers,
kale, black currant, and beans.

Hold It

Sometimes I think this, our life on earth, is an egg
to break out of ...
                                            —Susan Mitchell

Stand in the corner between couch and hearth,
where maidenhair fern overhangs

the black figurines captured shining,
domestic in a dollhouse jungle.

Pose there between your sisters, blink
a thousand times over.

Or on the front step, in a screen-door frame,
geranium planter buttressing the sides.

Tallest to shortest in matching skirts,
hair sausage-curled and beribboned.

What was that woman telling herself, what
question were we three the answer to?

Rare snap of my father in a summer shirt,
dangling a string of fish, biggest to small.

❧

Her hold over me a grey cloud, weight
that smothers. To save myself I exhale

a bubble of air, a shell in a snowdrift. Ah.
She's got me now. Limited vision. We

will do everything over and over till meaning
loses itself or makes; she will take me apart.

Avalanche of years, same bubble.
I survived, but where's the joy in that?

        🖋

In the middle of joy is an egg.
It has no legs. Its meaning

the same meaning over and over;
to change will deny

that in the beginning was the word.
Or was it the world?

The word fixed, the world fluid.
Inside the shell is the potent being.

        🖋

A shell is what makes a really good egg.
Like compressed talc, resilient and strong.

But eggs change as the chicken ages.
I could offer you perfect, over and over,

but then you wouldn't know about
Pearl, who lays an egg a day without rest,

small egg with a powdery shell, flawed
(who will care for it, keep it, attend?)

because despite her size she's low
on the totem pole of hens and will not

push her way to the best feed. I scatter
oyster shell before her; she ignores it.

Or Scrawny Buff, who settles
early every summer into broodiness,

drugged and irritable when I hoist her
mornings from the empty nest.

There are also the eggs of the old ones—
large, rich hue of milky coffee

but with scars of passage on them,
cirrus cloud, mares' tails.

You don't want to know this. You want
perfect, your own story, farm fresh.

❧

I could stand now, pick up the keys,
drive to town. I could take

three steps to the couch, lie down,
relax the pinched expression that cramps

my breathing passage. Victorian. Pinned
like an insect-that-was in a velvet case.

I could tip my head to a blade of sun, let music
crack my vertebrae. The breeze picks up.

Those street photographers of long ago; those
black-and-white snaps of our ancestors

striding a city street—that's what we want.
Hold it. Always followed by *Right*

there. Shadows puddle under
the Italian plums. Cloud lifts, the sky

floods blue. Sight ferries the soul
past the eggshell cornea, but then

(small egg, powdery flawed shell)
who will care for it, keep it, attend?

If we could slow the convergence of aging and winter—
(Avalanche of years, same bubble.)

But I'm new to this, and the point is convergence.
Show me how to hold time in both hands.

O great mother hen, be with me, be my shell;
roll us to the run's far corner where sunflowers

drop seed. I could study that dance. Together
we'll break and mend our hearts over and over.

Hold it. Always followed by Right there.

Sideways

When I moved here more than two decades ago
we bought our farm from the Johnsons,

but they'd owned it only three years
and had never moved in. We arrived midsummer

to repairs made on the foundation
and the base of the house scraped bare.

While I ran my gaze from the uncut field to an ailing
cherry to the well at the heart of the brambles

and inhaled deeply the direction my life was taking,
the young sons of a neighbour trailed a snake

over cracked earth and the caretaker chatted
about Africa, where he was headed in a month. So

my vision of what we were buying was
equatorial, parched, and reptile-haunted.

In fact we are part of the rainforest
and only garters and sharptails abound.

My point is no one else wears this
precise chain of perceptions, linked

charms braceletting a particular
piece of land.

When our sometime handyman Peter
hauled the woodshed upright and reroofed it,

he unearthed bricks from a kiln
that used to operate nearby, on Bricky Bay,

before either of us was born. And while he winched
the come-along, because the shed is on the road,

drivers stopped, among them a man who'd
lived in the house as a child and recalled

his father fifty years before, erecting
the "garage"—which, unbraced in time, slid sideways

until supported by surrounding trees.
My point is the land is still called

the old Mollison place, though I'm not sure
if the Mollisons lived here before the Johnsons

or before the owners before them.
It takes a long time to be recognized. As if

the island were peopled by all who ever
spaded the valleys or levelled ridges or stumbled

over shale. Once you're here long enough
you begin to see where each fits.

When you're here longer still
those who've passed begin to see you.

Relay

The days are handed off like bright batons.

A runner stutters into dark, the night
ahead. Ahead, dawn tucked beneath her arm,

someone else begins to hammer
the pulsing slope of mount grief,

while, in her wake, another navigates
the barberry thicket of what might

have been achieved. Who she was or will be
keeps her company the far side of the track,

winded, lurching forward, looking back.

A Short Time or Forever

I come by words honestly,
as if there are two of me.

One's happy with life—
how could I not be? The other

says, *You fool! How long
do you think this can last?*

Growing! Quick then to greet
the inconceivable. How could I

not be? My own yellow dress,
second-hand, I wore

in the months anticipating junior high.
I was eleven or twelve. First day

at the new school with sadness
I felt the zipper's straining teeth.

River Road

My mother, who has not walked without support
for more than a decade, who has dwindled

in height each winter and clasps, in passing,
the backs of chairs, the kitchen sink,

lifts her face from the coffee I've set
at her elbow to tell me again, make it

vivid, her dream: she is ten years old,
her rag-curled hair bound by a floppy bow.

At her back, under trees, the women in her family
picnic from a cloth spread to the coulee's edge.

Before the sun has dipped, her father will fetch them
in the Gray-Dort with its seats like skin

and curtained rear window. She stands on the brow
of a green slope flush with late-spring grass,

and when the Gray-Dort engine
purrs like a smug bumblebee from the river road

she looks up from her patent leather shoes rubbed
with Vaseline for gloss, and laughs, breathes in

the honey scent of balsam poplar's sticky leaves.
The sturdy machine of her heart propels her,

swoops her down into her life.

One True Thing

The Price of Nectarines

Weeks before my mother dies, I pack
my saddlebags with what I'll need—

lavender blanket, plastic flatware—

say farewell to the women who for years
shared tea on Tuesday afternoons.

Last, Mom, who cries when I confess
it won't be possible to phone;

whoever I'm fleeing, into the foothills,
may tap the line. But I've worked out a code.

I'll call one of her friends, those faithful
tea-drinkers, speak one sentence and hang up.

I'll say, for example: *Tell Nellie*
they raised the price of—

and whatever vegetable or fruit I name will share
the initial of the town I shelter in. In this way

cabbage equals Calgary; Edmonton, eggplant.

Not precise or personal, but she will know
that I'm all right, and may guess where. I unfold

this dream from my coat pocket on the day she dies.
I pull it out to make a note about the butterflies.

The floor lamp

was my grandfather's and lit
the armchair by the phone for all
my growing up, later weathered
rocky transport to the coast.

A week after my mother's death, I tip
the pole to dust its shallow
milk-glass top. The bowl slips loose
and smashes on the hearth.

Huge sorrow like a thundercloud
approaches—and passes over,
almost nothing. Comes to me then
how objects are loved most

through interference, our breaking
and mending, or seeing anew: new
shade, new light. How what we love's
loved least in its preserving.

Ecology and Ethics

Last night the fingers of my left hand brushed
the saffron velvet trousers of Prince Charles.

We were leaving a lecture, stepping down
to the classroom exit, and I sped up

to reach him at the door. Public buildings
are the size they are, I think, to echo

our relationship to aspects
of the world we've lost: old

trees, waterfalls, yawning canyons:
we're trying to return perspective

to the scraped bedrock of our lives.
The instructor ties a canvas sun hat on her head.

After class, because it was the last
and in honour of the Prince of Wales, tea.

Also leaving, and I knew she'd come
for royalty and not the lecture,

was my mother's old friend Mrs Hepple,
in a summer dress and high-heeled mules

like those she'd always worn and couldn't manage.
I held her arm as she stumbled to the tea tent,

then to the sideboard to get us both cups.
Things had been picked over by the end

of our careful walk. On paper cloths on the long tables:
trays of broken biscuits, crumpled napkins, stains.

I added to the mess by elbowing a flask of rum
set by the cream and lemon. I'd been reaching toward

two honey-glazed lozenges,
all that remained

of an apricot flan I hadn't known
I wanted.

Fishtail

How far from centre will stability extend?
Can one keep upright by her own drive?
Parked outside a Creston shop,
1938 painted green in the stucco front,

I'm reading *Paradise, Piece by Piece,*
waiting for coffee to kick in. In last night's
stuffy hotel room before sleep, I got Molly Peacock
from one marriage to another, not her own.

She had a schedule: from nine to noon she wrote poems;
afternoons she mailed them. In the evening
she fell in love with a dancer.

I want to stop being careful, but
not while I'm driving, not yet.

I want to know first what
the purpose is of caution, care. And trying

to figure out, in Molly's story,
how one enacts *eccentric* honestly, what it is
to make art in a family that resists more than it owns.

One betrays the first rule, which is
to follow the rules, to make stability
more stable.

And is blessed by the serendipitous.

Spin the dial to an interview with Molly Peacock,
who reads from her memoir, then a poem she wrote
after her mother died, about clip-on earrings.

My mother kept hers, two hundred pairs, all
flash and pick-me-up, like gemstone lures,
in a double of my father's tackle box.

Years ago when I sewed

rag dolls of both genders, my mother wanted
one. Now that she's dead I've inherited
the girl I gave her. My friend's daughter

calls it the Nellie-doll and plays with it
on visits. The dog would like to. In the dream
my husband takes the Nellie-doll to work.

On his return he shows me
what he's altered: rubber soles
on her cotton feet, rubber disks

where her breasts would be. How
do I feel? Has he transgressed
a compact? Do I inflate the signs?

Her face too has been re-embroidered,
near unrecognized. Whose
image here? It seems she has three eyes.

Vest

My mother walks better, or at least more quickly, but
this frightens rather than reassures. Through the window she
skirts the green lawn, like a statue on wheels

about to topple. My husband and I clean her basement.
She is again in residence, alive and alone; we are in town
to make more room, to simplify. It isn't going well,

too much stuff stored, not just the forgettable
remnants of my youth but what no one will ever talk about,
and I'm sad to be leaving, having impinged not at all. Here

are pieces of a garment I began sewing years ago:
a wine-coloured vest with dots on it like stars
and its wine-coloured lining, shapes unjoined,

without the tiny watchpocket-to-be
buttonhole-finished in the front panel.
Will I ever complete the project?

It will not travel to the coast with me, but
neither can I throw it out. I fold the envisioned
vest into a package, to be sheltered

in my mother's house a little longer.
I open my hand and stroke the dark
velvet of the separate shapes,

the small scattered truths that will not knit.

Out Of

Here in my hometown, the remnants
of family encamped, everything's clenched.

Muscles tight in my back—*fish, water,* how
ever survive?—tight in my jaw, even now.

My sister, who cared for our mother
her last months, other side of the country,

plays a video of that Christmas. In it, shadow
of her regal self, our mother declaims vaguely

over gifts. Wrenched, uprooted from the town
she watched grow up. Anyone's guess

how she felt. She died of maybe
not knowing, of realizing—out of her

element, her principled shuffle between table, TV,
bath, and bed—that she did not know.

A List of Allergies That May Include My Name

My mother lies in a hospital bed
with curtains drawn to enclose it:
ornate, multicoloured panels, weighty—
a canopy bed for old royalty.

I vacuum outside the enclave, stooping
to smooth the plum brocade. By her head
the drapes are an assortment of delicate prints.
When I finish, she wants the vacuum inside.

She can't say clearly where she would have
what she wants, and I move it twice
before plugging in near her left foot.

Then she's quiet; her face calms.
I wait outside—is this my place?—
and watch the billowing purple roar.

Remembering Summer

Later, on the ferry home, reading about
St Hubert's Mass, I can see the dogs.

In all the low-lit prairie towns I've left
they pad down dusty drives to congregate

and swarm the steps of old cathedrals.
Among them, the malamute-corgi cross

my mother leaned from her wheelchair to greet,
collarless haunt of the boulevard,

short-legged, blue-eyed, otherworldly soul
I was a little afraid of. He followed or led us

up streets I never thought my mother
in her nightdress would agree to go,

into Mrs Such's yard, where Mrs Such clipped
evening-scented stock, a bud of the flamingo rose

and spilled the flowers in my mother's lap
recalling, yes, a man

who may have had the same last name and was
unhappy with his wife.

That's how things go, she said;
her own son wasn't how she thought he should be either.

The one true thing, I knew, buckling my mother in:
she wanted me to fix her sadness, expected me to try.

I waited so long, she said. I know she did.
I opened my eyes to the second hand's shudder,

its epileptic spasm night and day, 1:42. At 1:42
the cog heaved itself through. If she dressed

I'd try to persuade her to let me push her chair
outside. Lilies on 16ᵗʰ Street, yellow poppies up the road.

She was lying down. I wanted
to rest too, five minutes only, but first

there was a pill she had forgotten, next the gardener rang
the bell. And how then could I settle while he

snipped and tugged at the foundation? I slid
a pan of Irish tea bread into the oven, waited it out.

My mother woke herself crying, continued. *Oh dear.*
Nothing to be done. The sky, a hard blue.

Her walker squeaked at the bathroom door. She spat
in the sink and breathed, *Oh dear,* some numbered exhalation.

She thought going out might be too difficult.
The radio played all night, the room stayed lit.

Satellites circled Earth, my heart flared at times, at others
cooled to the grey of weathered rock. Flat

on her back in the middle of the bed, head tipped,
mouth open. Country music rode out on her breath.

I must save my tea bag, she had a plan for it.
Raisins would soak in cold tea overnight. Tomorrow

will be Monday. There being no wind and no rain
she thought we might drive to the mall.

Since my last visit the wall clock
has shed its two-o'clock petal under the couch.

The more attractive she found the rice-paper napkins, a gift,
the more she lamented. Used, crunched up and not

looked at again. She would like them folded
and refolded gently—elevated, recollected, smoothed.

I waited so long, said my mother.

Things go, said Mrs Such.

The Hospital Bed, Again

She has just died, and when
my sister enters the room I tell her so.
We are still talking over her when she sits up.

I recall what the vet said under the plum tree:
that there might be spasms,
that we shouldn't confuse these

with movements of the living. So when
my mother groans, sits up, and asks
what is going on, is she not dead,

I tell her yes, she is,
and this seems to reassure her.
Wary, my sister leaves to find a nurse.

Since my mother is still with me, undiminished,
I take the opportunity to let her know

that her repeated impolite demands
to rub her feet and rearrange her gown
provoked my rage. I think it's time

to set things straight between us.
She regards me blankly, mildly puzzled.
I can see her wondering what earthly

use this information is, this detail
from another's head. After all, she's dead.
But won't lie down, not yet,

not till she's good and ready.

Bucket

Spirit beside the bird bath
in the fruit tree's dappled shade: so
unreachable now,

iconic. Apple and shrubs
a memory garden planted
for Muriel's dad. Is this what

happens? Does what we love accrete, more
vital and moth-frail, till all that remains
is a bucket of powdery wings?

Then the bucket decays.

Almost thirty years old, the photo's
gaudy colours: high summer lawn
a tended electric green. On it

my old dog, at ease and pink-tongued,
his clown face half black and half white. I was
newly adult. Speechless, he was silky-furred.

Over his head a laden bough. Eden
about to spill its promise: bath
a stone goblet, cupping fire.

Sixty

All my memories are getting old.

No longer able to dance and drink
after digging the garden beds, sometimes
not even entertaining that desire
but sitting in the porch armchair
and reading about stars.

Late afternoon I sit, the sun going in and out,

inadequate to dry my greying hair. I am ashamed
of the twenty extra pounds, soft belly,
hard pads of flesh that ride my hips.
I am ashamed of my shame.

There is no end to it.

The Afterlife

Geese fly over, six in a string, loop back
and drop to the field. Afternoon mist rising,
the cloud sits higher on the ridge: manifestation

of an apportioned heaven and hell.
(How the outer world vanishes
with a click of the inner light!)

Destination, perhaps, not for us entire
but for parts of the self. To hell with our wicked
impulse, our morbid fancy, ungenerous gesture.

Falling dark slips around me like oil
or eel jelly, neither house nor lights
proof against it. Which helps to explain

how the schism of the afterlife was garbled.
(And here the evening star crests the horizon!)
We still find it arduous to rise above ourselves.

It's a matter of how much of the self achieves grace.
To allow a vision of afterlife, we shed
private troubles, join what's vivid, like

(in the rain, to the myopic)
a string of coloured lights.

Invitation

At my desk this morning, spooning oatmeal, coffee
on the boil, Cassandra Wilson asking *Shall we dance?*
when from behind my computer screen sashays

the slowest doe

testing the drift with her articulate hoof
a mere ten feet from glass. Nor does she vanish
right away, but dawdles at the lowest of

three cedar stairs

twitching her mulish ears and sampling
my boot-scent on the wood, swivelling the wedge
of her head to mirrored effect, flirty

unhurried

before hefting her barrel-body's tawny rump
in my direction, setting her prints in snow,
one at a time, like bread crumbs, behind her.

Heaven (Oregon, 1993)

I entered because I heard music.
Also, there was a soft-eyed dog at the door, a Pyrenees,

and, off to the side, kitchen utensils in disarray and a shelf
of spine-broke cookbooks, one of which was Moosewood.

The waitress asked did I want the beer with the sailing ship
or the one with the bird. *Full Sail Amber,* I said.

On the menu was tofu rancheros with salsa verde,
no dairy, no eggs. It came with a vinegar-chile bite,

and beans overflowed the cobalt-rimmed plate.
Platters arranged on white linen. A person

female or male swaggered out of the dark
in an untucked blue tee, his immaculate hair

dipping insolent over her brow. Skinny,
big-footed. Here were things I didn't know

I'd missed. The pink ceiling blessing
the waitresses. Wooden booths open

to window greenhouses and pots of bloom.
A handsome man wearing Birkenstocks

and a long impeccable braid. Bill Bartels
with his guitar on a piano bench in the shade.

What to record in the heart's log?
What would I hold? The beer

I didn't try, BridgePort Blue Heron.
The Sweet Dreams sign in neon.

The way the slipshod waiters, wandering in
and out, left doors to the kitchen

open. Without doubt, the rose kimonos,
high on the wall as if wafted there, released.

How the woman, the dog's companion,
smiled before she knelt to slip the leash.

The calendar

turned to the men with the beautiful faces.
I'm sitting in the winter corner of the gold
brocade couch while Bulgarian women sing

of harvest, celebration. Outside
the steady rain depends a haze into the valley;
water drains the cluttered eaves. I realize

how vulnerable I am to April's unexpected
slight stroke of the shoulder—how it startles,
like a truck in the night or the shredding

of cloth. Spring says, *You look more alive
than I've ever seen,* and I look
away. Wisteria in leaf, clematis gesturing at air.

❦

When the drake lowered his sleek soft head
to the mink's breath, when he launched himself into

the tunnel of blacker dark that shattered
and splintered to stars in his neck, how alive!
His three or four years on the planet an idyll,

as nothing to this.

Stay a while. The curtain of rain is the same
pond-green as the cottonwood. If we walk out
before songs of celebration end, we may need

to take a shovel to the world, raw
and wounded. A long time since
we have been whole.

Change back, change back.
Failing that, be done quickly.

The apple trees save themselves but
promise much. Through the south window
low clouds of cherry, drifts of pear.

Like Calls

At the picnic table now, again, pea soup
and Simon Armitage's *Dead Sea Poems*,
a small doe clattering the decking to my left.
Hightails it, she does, down the beach.

Poetry, magnifying spirit, feeds us.
Literally, bite by bite. I read
a true voice, a heartfelt line, something
flickers in me like caffeine or lust. Meaning

of the words, my life, is deepened.
Lucy paces by the fire on Fisgard Street,
a generation of young men I've never met
enlists, the neighbour oversees a ewe give birth—

the leaping spirit in us called by that
without. Legerdemain with
words, what people mouth every day,
give scant attention to.

Something is thrashing the water: an otter, a rock.

Maggie Helwig says, *We breathe*
trouble and beauty. That pairing, yes,
human, what we are: troubled
as in never still, as in troubled water.

When I phone to say I'll be home tomorrow,
my husband's voice is absent in gaps.
Up half the night, what might he be
were he not tired?

We're pulled to the water, the doe, then me,
because it's alive, as we are
drawn
to fires to war to sun to flowering trees.

The sun vanishes

so utterly in winter. Alone
in the world, unhoused, all
that is green or once was

wizens to night, wearing at dawn
an exoskeleton of frost. It feels
wrong in my body that this is so.

Some part of me yearns
to gather what I can carry and walk south.

Yesterday I forked a bucketful of carrots.
No longer than two hours in the porch
and a bright patch of inner orange gleamed,

top of a muddy root newly gnawed,
three pellets of rat shit on the blanket
blocking cold at the foot of the door.

How could a rat get in? No noise
all evening, no springing of the trap.

In the evening dark, which pours
into the valley after four,
life is careful, solitary, drab.

I fill a box with cedar shakes discarded
from the roof, lug it to the woodshed,
wheel fir and fruitwood back.

I wake heavy-limbed and grateful
for the light. At noon, when the sky is brightest,
I scatter grain for the hens, and tomatoes,

fruit that bruised in the dark as it ripened.

Salt

Spewed from the glittering eight-lane tunnel of Xmas
the daylight of New Year palls. Winter takes up

a steady plowing of the air. Resist.
Think of the wind when it comes as not

aiming to strip you of all that holds meaning
but bringing you more of what it has touched. Yesterday's sky

was glorious, and when you hung sheets on the line
they snapped in the chill breeze. Then dusk,

the plow blade scours the slope, cleaving
what won't bend, hurling debris at the window.

Times the plow blade roars and you roar back.
Between whoops the landscape falters, pales. I waken

feeling, if not anxious, low. Uncertain
of my worth, and far from joy.

Frost last night, a shimmer of it over the field,
and in the sky a haze, the air particulate.

Buttercup

Made a list of uncompleted stanzas
assembled on my desk in paper clips.

Read Garrison Keillor's intro to
Good Poems, and the first section.

Drank my weight in tea, moved on
to a flask of Jameson's I keep upstairs,

haunted only by Ray Carver wanting
one more day.

The rain has stopped; occasional
rats rustle in the walls. Downstairs

our dog demands a meal and gets it.
A goldfinch bobs and settles in the field,

masquerading as that weed that wanders,
seeds itself, and thrives. Yellow,

frog-family for articulated leaves.
Likes damp. Infiltrates grass. I turn

the pages of a French country diary,
a friend's gift years ago. Out of date,

never more than tidbit for the urban soul
with money for hired minions, rural

dreams, no matter, the images
still pull me: powder-blue wheelbarrow,

peony dropping its petals. Morning follows
evening. Casual. Precise.

Mowing

On Friday Karl spiralled the field on his tractor,

mowing the June-high grass to a carpet of green
that over the next days silvered in the heat.

He arrived again, towing a gang of rakes that hooked
and flung the hay, and the day after that

towed the chunky baler, folding and stuffing the wiry stems
into a maw that ka-chunked and spat them transformed.

Ninety-eight bales threw sunset shadows in the field.

Before dark, two pickups entered the lower gate
and crawled west. Beside them the labourers walked,

tossing the bales to the truck bed, where one of them sorted
and stacked. The courses rose by the minute, and the stacker,

while, laden, the vehicles sank on their axles.
Forty bales per truck, I figure, in maybe a half hour.

All that had surged to shoulder height in a season
was stowed and wheeled away, steamer trunks

of weather and trauma, coincidence, time, gone
to be winter's meal for soft-mouthed sheep.

The bales appeared to rise of their own accord
from the workers' hands. I know what a bale weighs.

Water and soil conspire to multiply, to occupy
a breathing space above the field.

This is magic. Then comes night and a smattering
of rain, broadcast from the scudding clouds.

In the morning a haze of new leaf.

The Fields Renew

Sometime after enough
heat, light, wind

the trodden meadows
plump up, achieve
an overfed, complacent look

until awestruck by winter.

And there, again: the bones
of the land, the sunken scars

where rivulets in spring
washed daffodils
in flawless swaths downhill.

The hedgerows move, slow
armies, year by year;

the brambles kneel,
hawthorn and rose recover
the front lines. After a killing frost

the fields renew, clean
and sweet beneath a common sky.

Flutter

In a blue plastic chair under the apple tree the farmer
sits, bucket between boots, a little water in it,
and wraps the hen in a towel to secure her wings and feet.
Tipped slightly, the hen is calm and quiet.

When I checked the flock at noon, the old girl we call Dora
was no worse, but the egg-bound red had sickened
and been pecked about the head and comb.
I lifted her over the fence into Dora's pen,

but the flies found her, and for the next few hours
she merely rowed her heavy body onward. Now
the farmer makes a diagonal slit and holds
the hen's red head while she bleeds out.

Before he cuts the farmer strokes
her head and neck, surprising us
with a song he possibly made up
about great mother and the sky and wings.

In the middle of the day, after finding the red
with her damaged comb, I cried, not only
for the red hen's wretchedness but also
Dora's slow demise, the weed-throttled

garden's caving fence, our untended house—
its peeling paint and rotting roof—an inability
to foster or preserve what's in our care.
There's a flutter at the end, not much,

held by the towel and the farmer's hand.
When she's gone I empty the bucket into compost.
We find the least-packed soil in the field near the run
and in the shadow of the loft begin to dig.

The Long View

We're-all-here-to-see calls some night bird
early, cloud closing in. But it's

evensong, over by sleep. We all sleep;
Earth sleeps, the moon. Still,

progress needs to measure where it's been.
I cross the salt dunes, look back

at the numbered pillars. This coast:
once Spanish, then British—it happens—

now all-out America. Families of three
have a total age less than forty, and fathers

heft cameras like a second head.
To see; but how much seeing can one do?

&

In the black night the silver flare
of what I believed to be my dying sight

arced like a comet falling east. I leaned
through a tent flap, stripped of expectation.

I see, I said. Then the sound of that, shattering.

&

Let's take the long view—melodramatic, true.
Standing upright renders us more

visible, permits us to see farther.
On the beach, candles planted against

the wobbly dark. Do you see
what I mean?
                    Sight

has collared us, hauled upright,
hammered of us an axle
                                between

salt flats and the wheeling
stars.

                    ✍

My dog is a hunter, almond eyes
needling a thread to the far bead

of an eagle over the ridge or the flick
of a deer tail in the valley brush.

Deep-chested and lean; the snick of her jaws
has felled a goldfinch on the wing.
                                        Wings

open in a sign of absolution.
The field is bright and cold. The air

bores tunnels in the brain. Every day
she carries my heart to me in her teeth.

❧

The pen leaves the page; my gaze
veers to the middle distance.

From root and fur sight wrenched us. Here:
a strange place; I don't live, and how

much seeing, in any case, can I do?
It's all right, I murmur, *all right.* You know

that late afternoon distress, when coffee wears off
or lack of food sets in: you're far from home.

❧

Walking on two legs rather than four
released our bodies from the constraints

of the synchronized breathing gait that so many
other animals, such as dogs and horses, live by.

Once the lungs of our two-legged ancestors were freed,
they could modulate their breathing in subtle ways

that may have contributed to the evolution
of speech.

❧

Ah,

the sun, a whiskey burn
behind the lids.

I see, I say. I see. Every day
my heart to me in her teeth.

Snow Globe

Early morning. Won't be long.
My collie elbows her cushion, alert, signalling time

for a meal. We dreamed deep together,
back to back, and now the morning dawns ... pellucid?

Is that the word? Calm, unshadowed by regret or rain,
sheltered from midday's unforgiving light.

Fog surrounds the ridges like a dome,
as if the valley were whittled in coral

or built of balsa: tiny house, toy woodshed,
miniature sheep piled to one side

of the matchstick paddock awaiting crumbs.
Now my girl grunts at me: get up, go down.

All creatures hunger for the day. Though it
(as they) begin and end as yesterday, all

creatures want wholly
to be in it.

A Few Notes, Maybe

Before I got up this morning I cried.

Life: a cruel joke. As if having heard
the breathtaking precision of its speech,
we are given an instrument
we don't know how to play.

I dressed. Now I drive to the ferry, plucked
by the need to organize, consolidate,
come at things differently: what
flares, what travels, what might occur.

Sheep in a line have jumped a gate and graze the shoulder.

Categories, sub-categories, timelines, tasks.
Is it natural for humans to be moral? Either
we are one with nature
or, because we're moral, we're not.

Once again, I'm certain. Tuned. Everything
came down the road. Now: a man in a black beret,
onions tied to the grips of his bike.
Valhalla? Bagged, on the coast road.

Vidalia. Spanish onions. French beret.

Empty Suet Cage

Inside, I dreamed of constellations—
those feeding creatures outlined by stars,
their skeletons a darkness between jewels,
heroes that exist only where they are not.
                              —William Stafford

Uncut, the canary grass rises up blond.
I sat at the window, overlooked
the growing dark, at home
in the betwixtness. Refusing to commit
to nightfall, when I might
turn on the lamp, get on with work, give up
the outside chance.
Inside, I dreamed of constellations—

without electric light the sky still blooms.
And an hour ago, when it seemed the wind
was going, gone, the hens stepped out
and swarmed the gate, awaiting
company, a fist of scratch. The small birds too
rained down; I scattered seed,
refuelled the empty suet cage,
those feeding creatures outlined by stars,

when once the wind has dropped. And my mind
begins to sweep small
dust piles of intent, perceptions. Wider the reach
in both directions. Deep breaths. The alders
sway like warning fingers,
their skeletons a darkness between jewels.

I want to do
nothing but read a novel under a blanket by the fire.
I want not to be
there. Here. The dust piles
accumulate. Is what we say goodbye to
the world and the flesh? Or the bond
of brain and time? Strung between the two like
heroes that exist only where they are not.

The Last Straw

When talk of sleet postponed my paperwork upstairs,
a phrase arrived that perfectly signified
something. Gone now. Something to do
with giving up or in, acquiescing, knuckling under.

Last night's first of three predicted storms was merely rain
and a stiff breeze. Tonight the second tries us.
Saturday the tail of a typhoon may grind us flat.

The poem the phrase unfolded would address
my husband's injured leg, the tumbled plum,
our lame hen's pirate shuffle, bean trellis twisting
and plummeting like a compass point in a storm.

Under the pall of forecast rain I dug two garden beds, mowed.
I raked up the last of the bales and mulched what I could.

At Long Last

I've finished gleaning Robert Hass's
apple trees, less satisfying than the fruit

of smaller, source collections
too expensive to reprint.

I've poured hot rum and set
the cup atop the radiator to warm;

I've doused the lamp
and lit a candle on the sill.

At solstice I knew where I stood—
in the torque of too much, and therefore

meaningless, save in relation to.
Now the outer world is visible again,

fog like wet muslin hooked in the trees.
More than a minute a day now.

A kinglet or bat tips from the roof,
arrows into the valley's current.

The sun has driven its narrowest edge,
begins to pry open the dark.

End of the Decade, Already Dark

I remove screens and shades
from my study windows, and the glass

excepting one barn light sends back
an image of the room. Near my feet

the dog after much grumbling agrees
to settle so long as I'm perfectly still.

Here's what I scribbled last week in bed,
after getting up in the cold dark to pee:

Nights I sleep alone I take my measure,
small, dry against the yellow field of sheet.

The donkeys have munched apples
and an evening arm of hay; the chickens

are shut up, aroost. The neighbouring cows
shoulder into line along the gate. They wait.

They dredge a heartfelt chorus of why
the entire wagonload of bales

should be heaved across the wire.
I drink a second mug of tea. Near five thirty

cold permeates the wall.
Tail lights flash; the frenzied mooing

stills. Lights pull away. Each day
I plan how the next will differ,

will more resemble what
I want a life to be.

III

First Marriage

Side by side at the cafe's outdoor table,
my husband with calculator, I with pen, we

try to reckon the affording of our lives.
On the one hand. On the other. There

is what comes in, and what might.
The money that's gone and is going.

The inexcusable luxury of so much unproductive land.
Robin in the uncut grass, beak stuffed with worms.

A warm morning in early June on our island,
and we're at war until something

gives up or gives in. How all those tiny words
propose essentially the same.

It is helpful, meanwhile,
to have a topic. What I believe

is sunlight on its way to butter,
on the tongue of the thoughtful cow.

The waitress hums as she refills our cups.
At the next table with great animation

a couple turns pages of an album; she asks
again and again, *And who's this?*

I'm not who you think I am, you know. Not even
who I think I am. My husband blinks.

This morning a fledgling trapped itself
in the duck yard, panicked, flapping and falling

against the patchwork fence. The gaps,
vast as they are, invisible. The old ones

shrieked me up from the garden
to open the gate.

Burning Bush

We stopped in the yard at a kind of lilac
that bore no bloom but red berries instead.
And out of the leaves, which were coppery too,

propelled a prehistoric bird, like a kite
made of wood, rippling and rattling its bony tail.
What is that colour called, like dried blood?

&

I think about an earlier, brief affair. How we
are drawn to someone, then find ourselves
mistaken in the pull. Could be

neither person nor place is wrong
but time: we open to who this one
has been, might be, give or take a dozen years.

&

What if nostalgia's launched not by experience,
but lack? Could be it recalls one's absence. Could be
one never feels such loss if one was wholly

there. Sufficient unto the leaf
is the breeze thereof. Aspen. Aspire. Unto
berries the blood. Thereof the astonishing

bird, whose tail joints, mountain ranges, shift,
whose wings clap the air and sift
absurdities,

which settle on the upturned brow.

        🍂

The randomness of life, is what he said.
Do not attempt to hang from the towel, or insert
your head in the loop. Look what we've

got: Sufficient unto the ＿＿ is the ＿＿ thereof. Memory
fled. Not carmine, magenta, maroon. Akin
to indigo. That which ignites the back of the neck.

Small Potatoes

for Michael

Between us

and our elderly neighbours, a picket fence.
His name escapes me. Hers we never knew.

He said, *Don't buy; the house is old.*
And yet he seemed pleased when we did,

pleased for the several summers till
we remarked a lengthy quiet, a flush

of weeds and afterward, the sign—*For Sale.*
Till then, once he knew

we ate them unpeeled, with salt and butter,
he'd line potatoes on the picket fence,

fresh dug—too small, he said,
for him to bother with.

Between us,

our house was small, without
foundation, slated for demolition

more than once. Had been
constructed half a century before

for parents of cigar-store owners
who lived next door. Since then

added to, encumbered. Like a camel it
heaved itself to its feet at any passing dream

of home. Remember how tricky
aligning wallpaper stripes in that room?

Framework collapsing decade by decade,
closet opening askew. But what a beguiling

print: straws of green and lavender and
blue. I panicked in the kitchen,

first autumn, ironing—
ironing!—while you worked overnight.

How was I deep enough in this coupling
to share a house? At the juncture of four rooms,

walls curved, announced themselves
a hall. There I painted a stone hearth,

a steady fire; on the elbow of night sky
I thumbed glow-in-the-dark stars.

Later the living room would house
caged birds, and after that

just cages, but in the first winters an evergreen
regaled the northeast quarter, and once,

friends, sleeping over to hang baubles,
woke with the twinkling tree in their laps.

Their baby snuffled, slept. In our tiny house
that night, eight people lay.

Which Christmas was it you gave me
a porcelain cottage, emblem

of what we might build? Underground
electric: its perfect lamplit charm.

Our first refrigerator, lined in pink—
the motor woke us nightly.

                    Between us

the new linoleum, patterned close as could be
managed to Dutch tile. Blood on the quilt,

my aging dog's thinning blood. We
doused flying ants with bleach one August.

Comfrey wouldn't take. The weeping
birch travelled. Salamanders

revealed themselves each May
in the brick planter over which we hung

the caged canary. His tropical voice
recalled the finches every spring.

                    Between us

a small yard, sumac and blackberries, all
the templates of family. I wanted

to jackhammer asphalt. No going back
from that. I wanted our own

potatoes. My old dog, cornered
by the neighbours' toddler, bit.

The child beneath the fallen tinselled tree
grew, married, was widowed before thirty.

My dog who padded those rooms
and the four sidewalks of the block

moved with us to be buried. The hardy
fuchsia was uprooted too, and a young

weeping birch now emulates
the neighbour's winding drive.

The house itself we sold to friends
who birthed a daughter there.

Between us

the glass-fronted cabinet a friend built,
the desk lamp that lit my grandfather's books.

Blue-eyed trellised morning

glory on porch walls.
The deep

footed porcelain tub.

Skilsaw

In the last year of our marriage my husband
rose early. One July morning I fell back
into sleep, and dreamed of a pair of men,

scientists, doctors in lab coats, methodically
placing a saw at the side of my head.

Pointing, narrating the process. Beginning
above the right ear, with debate between them:
when to veer to the top of the skull, when deep.

I could feel the teeth cold on my skin,
could not believe in any way out but

out. At that point I became someone else,
paler, smaller-voiced, slipped through the lower
half of the dutch door. I looked for help.

Basement of a five-storey house, no one
home on any floor, and I kept climbing.

Night Visitor

Last night in town I slept lightly,
woke often from three until dawn, mistaking
the small metallic rustle—mouse in the wall—
for my husband's key in the lock.

I dreamed a tall stranger
entered the basement room.
Neither alone nor afraid I
might have been watching a film, turned

to check with my companion
about the actor's name. The tall man,
he said, though on the side of good
was a loose cannon, known to display

the hole in his plexus,
size of a dinner plate,
his own energy had razed.
He could appear too with wings,

enormous sails an angel might wield,
but tawny and grey like an owl's.
While I awaited my husband's return,
contemplated mouse whispers,

the tall man guided my companion.
Or did he do the work himself?
A nuclear device disarmed:

four blinking lights extinguished
and we
one by one, that might
have ignited the world.

Bearing

Toward morning wind rattles the glass, breaking
the dream in which I had two sons. One
died young. The other was named Lander.

Into a hole for safekeeping went my bright-eyed
boy, my beauty, he who could swim like a fish,
who sang, and played with fire. I wander through

the spare room night houses extend into,
and find my blond son with another child
he will not introduce. In time I recognize

his brother's ghost, but grown, the age
he would have been had he survived.
I calm myself. Though staggered by the strange

course of my life, I'm coping;
mothers do. In the spare room
with my children, I think this through.

The son I know, a guide to one I don't, is fluent—
the disordered words, the crablike walk!—
and willing, once I navigate my wonder

at realizing the two have met for years.
Of course. Lander's a lonely, loving child and drawn
to play. To the unmanaged. We all

know what's allotted won't suffice. But can I trust this other
boy who's grown up not among the living? Whose gaze
meets mine and skitters sideways, glittery, marine?

He knows no earthly laws. And clearly death
does not concern him. But he's a child. Perplexed,
I smooth my skirt, breathe deeply in the murk

and choose to trust my living son, who eyes us,
curious, car in hand, over the cloverleafs
and interchanges of his racetrack set.

Trapline

for my father

I'm content to sit alone at my high window,
watch white drifts dissolve on earth. Even
the rain. Even long puddles that tatter the field.

Wind has loosed its hold on our necks.
Rain slows, a rattle on the roof. I'm reading
a pantoum about John Thompson hunting

and think of you: *What you find in the morning,*
you skin and feed off of all winter. And though
the poet may be wise to see memory as *part bullet,*

and though an editor might excise that *of,*
the line resonates—a trapline shimmers:
your desire, but also mine, for day's work

to be simple and what nourishes, to live
hand to mouth. At its best, an offering;
worse, penitence. Tracking the injured.

The cedar posts gleam red against wet green;
the poplars wear a haze of the new season.
Meditation, a way of staving off despair.

Convalescence

I bribe the dog with a biscuit, and we both
take up spots on the divan. Thin cloud veils
the sun, and cool wind dries the morning mist.

Averse to taking up my pen, I've been
afraid to fix on nothing. I was looking
for an idea of note, a sign of my own intelligence.

Yesterday, thunder. Great cracking rolls of it.
John Banville has Copernicus discover
on his deathbed: the world,

which is the point, and its mundanities. Memory
fragmented, scrappy, like old lace.
Then clarity of mind. With health comes agitation.

I say to myself, *How long can you lie incapable?* Or no,
unwilling. Banville's Copernicus hoards his work
till the end. I drink a second cup of tea and feel it

shimmer in my heart. Bird in the hand.
The world is all, the world and our longing.
Children leave the school bus to walk

the sunlit road, raised voices free of words. They
mean nothing. How good
it feels to write this—not joyous, not only,

but an ease of anxiety, as if someone
has been saying, *Pay attention.*
As if writing were an act of listening.

Yesterday I believed, reading Rumi,
that everything is god, that I
should walk into morning with that as a mantra.

But I didn't. Nevertheless the trees
shout their holiness; impossible to be deaf to it.
Pasture, the green sun made edible. The cows come

late afternoon to the cool of cottonwoods,
the bull and nine cows and a half-grown calf.
They lower their heavy bodies into puddles of calm.

After Illness

When last did I exhale such
gratitude? If not whole, I am at least

a little like myself. Today a quarter moon
of cantaloupe appeals, the ache

retreats from eyes, neck,
lower back, and lungs.

Sufficient to stroll with my husband
through Bolen Books, impress

the full sole of each foot
heel to toe in the shining aisles,

recognize the shoddy map my brain's
become, needing the links: What is

the book I read and liked
about the chronometer? Who wrote it?

What did she also write concerning
a father-scientist and letters?

And thus with my husband's help I get
to *Galileo's Daughter,* and then

across campus to Lucy. Old friends, we
eat pea soup, nod to my sentimental state,

rest a little in the sun. Now here I am,
back to a sun-warmed wall, in the grass

beneath my husband's office window.
Just when I'm too hot, a breeze

bestirs; the shrubbery's alight:
forget-me-nots, day's-eyes.

Equinox

Because the day promised sun, I washed
the bedding early, helped my husband tote
the futon, folded in half like a copy book, to drape
over the picnic table and take the air.

At two, the clouds moved in and threatened rain.
And so we lugged the bed back in—mattress cover,
sheets and pillow slips—and then the sun
breathed out again, burned back the shelf of cloud.

The sun shines now across my lap. Some time
after four and on the uphill side of six, I cradle it.

Donkey Walk

Yesterday morning after the dust of ferry traffic settled
we walked the donkeys to their new home.

The trek took less than an hour and was sadly easy.
Such a well-behaved pair, so trusting, even eager,

save for a moment halfway where the younger
stalled, overwhelmed by the unfamiliar—

bags in the ditch, a yellow road sign, poodle
in a passing car, agape at the rear window.

Why had we not walked them every week,
and to the fair each August?

Daisies and poppies bobbed in the fields.
Two little girls with their mother and grandmother

hied from the library lot to stroke noses.
Drivers slowed and pointed, grinned.

But the face that came home with me and stayed
was an old man's, leaning from the passenger seat,

seeing only the donkeys, not us, his grey eyes
drunk with a past remembered.

When we set out, Snowman took the lead
to show Rufus all was as it should be,

and when Rufus grew rattled and overwrought
we let him pass on the inside. Speed

is an exaggeration. Sturdy beasts, they plodded,
tiny hooves on asphalt clacked a high-heel sound.

Are they going to new pasture? the library women
asked, and we said yes. It was true. A glorious walk

on a sunny morning in early July, seven years
less two days from their first grazing of our land.

Then we didn't know that they would age us,
laying their shaggy heads in our laps in summer,

shivering in icy wind, blanketed,
rolling the rain from their sodden coats in spring.

❦

Today the paddock gate is still ajar,
ribbons of fencing let fall in the grass.

All night I kept waking from a sky's
horizon pierced by evergreens,

a mile out of sync with my bed.
Where did they settle at nightfall?

Did they lie or lock knees? Someone else's
hands pour mash into the rubber bowl.

Let them be happy, and comfortable, and loved.

Let me see them soon.

The winter of her fourteenth year

I care for Sal. We stroll, and eat,
and read and doze. She dreams, her frail

hind legs kick hard enough, it seems,
to wake her, though then she's

deepest under, running summer-
wild and in pursuit, apparently,

of cat or deer. The kicks replay
her full-tilt race at evening

from donkeys to the house steps,
from my hand to my husband's,

soft fly-mask in her teeth, aloft
it seems with pleasure at having

in that moment grasped
we speak her language: our feet too

have kissed the crossing point
of work with joy.

Power Cut

I boiled a kettle on the camp stove, filled a thermos,
climbed up to light a candle against the looming dark.

No power. Noon wind from the southwest scoured cloud
high overhead, dipped low enough to fell a tree somewhere.

At least no rain, no ongoing overnight wild storm.
My husband's here, there's kindling in the woodbox,

no sick hens, a cache of books. This morning I combed
the beach, returned with a trug of sea lettuce.

It was a fine warm day with sun in it.

Close to five and I write by candlelight. With luck
tomorrow morning or the next, sun will dry the hoophouse walls

and we can mend them. My husband, leaning on his stick,
considers the south fence. Our collie inhales dusk.

The only lights betoken planes and cars. Fir and alder
wave tips at the horizon, not static, as you might suppose—

shade in winter courses the garden now. I pinch the taper,
ignite the pillar, which throws more light but less directly,

hold onto horizon's last glow—that band between the fir-lined ridge

and glowering cloud. Not scudding now, it's settled in.
The treetops barely move. The after-storm, when storms

no longer matter. All past hens in their below-ground nests:
Pearl and Barney, Adrienne, sweet Dora, the nameless

Reds, the hens I can't remember. Who is remembered, no matter
how many fragment-haunted beings try? Since the day of the dead

we've fired the string of lights that ornaments the plum.
Not this afternoon but mostly, nights, it glitters.

In the west, an eye of light: a cloudy pupil. Across it, silhouette
of a tree I strain to recognize. Is it near and unfamiliar? Or far and
    tall?

Its crown drags down the dark. It bridges.
The pupil of cloud closes. The iris, soul, awakes to what?

to wit? to anything? Hold on, hold open. Let's just watch and listen:

There might be more, the possibility of more. And then *again*
would alter what's perfected: lid of cloud, cheekbone of earth,

closed pupil of enough—that tree I hadn't noticed. On this land
a handful of decades and something grew, transformed

the frame. Until the power died I could not see it.

Quarter to six now, and the pupil-cloud, once negligible, is
gone: long triangle of light over the ridge, pushed up against

that tree I can't locate in daily life. No matter. Daily
life is inside now: the windup clock ticks ten to six,

a candle, honey-scented, flame subdued.
No need to talk about it anymore: the narrow

wedge of sky, horizontal shades, a striped alignment
of the grey. We grid the real. We have to, couldn't see it

otherwise. The poem lives in that hazy twilit

strip. I'm grateful, given that.
And when it's gone I'm grateful for what's inward.

Quiet, save the measure. A mild roar,
wind, an engine. Alders waving right, then left. That blurry

triangle of cave light forecloses fast now, all the fir-tips nosing
definition on the grid of the horizon when it goes.

I watch it. Sliver of the end of day. Today's
hope, for tomorrow. Inside: light,

the honey glow, the small.

Late

The valley thick with lethargy today: sun-hot
wind. A drowsy cricket whinge.

My husband lay an hour in the hammock
imagining potato salad into bowls.

Our Barnevelder died this week. Blue-banded
matriarch of the flock, she quieted,

tucked
               her head beneath her wing.

I've buffed and sorted fingerlings for market;
the coolers packed: zucchini, mesclun, cukes.

In boxes in the dark north room, ripe peppers
and Italian plums.

                     Time again
to go downstairs. I stalled ascending. As if

there were nothing to say. As if the same
could not bear repeating: food, light,

call of the sheep down the valley. Breeze
a gesture drawing the world's face, walnut

leaves
             a glittering green lake.

The Gleaners

Wendell Berry writes of his great-uncle's great-

grandfather's house, and Seamus Heaney of the place
that birthed him. That loving of the land

I understand, but not the land
loving me.

I special-order a bean called Red Swan
and one Silver Cloud cannellini: union
of the pragmatic and the winged.

Open a calendar. January prods
with a fox's face: inquisitive,
its pure self burning in the snow.

What recurs is soul—which,
not animal, ani-
mates. Mitch stirs

the rice, chops carrots and spuds. I turn
laundry by the woodstove, baking all sides.
Food ready, we'll watch *The Gleaners and I,*

touching, he says, on agriculture, scavenging,
aging and painting.
French, though; he warns me of that.

Yesterday after dishes and breakfast
I walked Sal round the loop. We sauntered
down Hooson to greet the horned sheep.

There was a moment at Hope Bay,
near the rushing culvert: a flicker
cried to my right and wood ducks skidded
a landing to my left.

I felt anchored in the world. Not solid but shining.
Another small ringing bell.

Acknowledgements

My gratitude to the Canada Council for the Arts for its support during the writing of these poems.

My thanks to John Barton for his attentive and generous work on the manuscript. The exchange of ideas and responses was a pleasure.

"Buttercup" and "Sideways" were previously published in *The Fiddlehead* and "Heaven (Oregon, 1993)" in *Arc Poetry Magazine*. Thank you to the editors.

"One True Thing" is for my sisters.

In the following poems I quote or allude to the words of other writers:

"Moving House": Roo Borson's words are from "California Nutmeg" in *Rain; road; an open boat* (McClelland & Stewart, 2012).

"Hold It": The epigraph is from Susan Mitchell's long poem "Bird: A Memoir" in *Erotikon* (HarperCollins, 2000).

"Like Calls": Maggie Helwig's words may have been spoken rather than written, since neither she nor I can locate them. She believes them to be a paraphrase of the lyrics of songwriter Carolyn McDade's "Trouble and Beauty."

"The Long View": The italicized section is from the preface to Craig Stanford's *Upright: The Evolutionary Key to Becoming Human* (Houghton Mifflin, 2003).

"Empty Suet Cage": The epigraph is from "A Message from the Wanderer" in *Ask Me: 100 Essential Poems of William Stafford* (Graywolf, 2014).

"Trapline": The italicized phrases are from Sue Goyette's "A Late Horizon" in *Undone* (Brick Books, 2004).

"The Gleaners": The film we watch is a documentary by Agnès Varda.

Born and raised in Lethbridge, Alberta, Marlene Cookshaw studied writing at the University of Victoria and later worked in various capacities, including for several years as the editor of *The Malahat Review*. Her poems have won several awards, among them the Ralph Gustafson Poetry Prize and the Robinson Jeffers Tor House Prize for Poetry. She has published six collections, five of them with Brick Books, including *Shameless* (2002) and *Lunar Drift* (2005), and in 2008 was presented with the Victor Martyn Lynch-Staunton Award for outstanding achievement in mid-career. She lives on a small farm on one of BC's southern Gulf Islands with her husband, fellow poet Mitchell Parry.